MEAT AND FISH HEALTHY AIR FRYER

WITH LOVE BY CATHERINE B. ROBERTS

Best Recipes Collection

To My Family. Thank You So Much For Supporting Me.

With Love, Catherine

Best Recipes Collection

© Copyright 2021 - All rights reserved. The content contained within this book may notbereproduced, duplicated or transmitted withoutdirectwritten permission from the author or thepublisher.Under no circumstances will any blame orlegalresponsibility be held against the publisher, or author,forany damages, reparation, or monetary loss due totheinformation contained within this book. Either directlyorindirectly.

Legal Notice:This book is copyright protected.This book is only forpersonal use. You cannot amend,distribute, sell, use,quote or paraphrase any part, or thecontent within thisbook, without the consent of the authoror publisher.

Disclaimer Notice:Please note the information contained within this document is for educational andentertainment purposesonly. All effort has been executedto present accurate, upto date, and reliable, completeinformation. No warrantiesof any kind are declared orimplied. Readers acknowledgethat the author is notengaging in the rendering of legal,nancial, medical orprofessional advice. The contentwithin this book has beenderived from various sources.Please consult a licensedprofessional before attemptingany techniques outlined inthis book.By reading this document, the reader agrees thatunderno circumstances is the author responsible for anylosses,direct or indirect, which are incurred as a result of theuseof information contained within this document,including,but not limited to, — errors, omissions, orinaccuracies.

Best Recipes Collection

Table Of Contents

Introduction	10
Why You should choose Air Fryer	13
How much should you eat?	14
What is air Fryer?	16
Tips for Cooking	17
101. Lamb Burgers	19
102. Lamb Spicy Lemon Kebab	20
103. Lamb Kofta	22
104. Easy Lamb Chops With Asparagus	24
105. Golden Lamb Chops	25
106. Lahmacun	26
Pork	**28**
107. Classic Southern Pork Chops	28
108. Original Herb Crusted Chops	29
109. Country-Style Pork Ribs	30
110. Dijon Pork Tenderloin	31
111. Pork Burgers with Red Cabbage Slaw	33
112. Parmesan-Crusted Pork Loin	35
113. Crispy Breaded Pork Chop	36
114. BBQ Pork Ribs	38
115. Super Meatballs	39

Best Recipes Collection

115. Seasoned Pork Chops	41
116. Spiced Pork Shoulder	42

Lamb   44

117. Greek Lamb Pita Pockets	44
118. Crusted Rack Of Lamb	47
119. Lamb Burgers	49
120. Lamb Spicy Lemon Kebab	50
121. Lamb Kofta	52
122. Easy Lamb Chops With Asparagus	54
123. Golden Lamb Chops	56
124. Lamb Loin Chops With Horseradish Cream	58
125. Lamb Rack With Pistachio	60

Fish and seafood   62

127. Tuna Burgers	62
128. Flavorful Baked Halibut	64
129. Glazed Tuna And Fruit Kebabs	65
130. Tender & Juicy Cajun Cod	67
131. Shrimp Skewers	68
132. Classic Scallops	70
133. Spicy Orange Shrimp	72
134. Tasty Parmesan Shrimp	74
135. Seafood Spring Rolls	76
136. Rosemary Garlic Shrimp	78

Best Recipes Collection

137. Roasted Halibut Steaks With Parsley	79
138. Fired Shrimp With Mayonnaise Sauce	81
139. Greek Cod With Asparagus	83
140. Halibut Steaks With Parsley	85
141. Roasted Scallops With Snow Peas	87
142. Air Fryer Salmon	89
143. Perfect Baked Cod	90
144. Spicy Grilled Halibut	91
145. Salmon Beans & Mushrooms	92
146. Salmon Cakes	93
147. Lobster Lemon Kebab	94
148. Fish Spicy Lemon Kebab	96
149. Coconut Shrimp	98
150. Lemon Salmon	99
My Secrets To Get Better Dishes and... Extra Crunchies	100
MEASUREMENT CONVERSION	104
Conclusion	**105**

Best Recipes Collection

Best Recipes Collection

Introduction

Are you a diabetic who loves to cook? Your dear needs to pay attention to sugar intake in his/her diet and you need a guide?

This book is specially designed for people with diabetes who want to enjoy delicious food without worrying about the consequences.

You can have a normal life and enjoy any event now!

I will show you how easy it can be to make your favorite dishes and even some new ones that are healthier than ever! You'll also learn how to read labels, what foods are safe, and which ones might not be so good for you.

There's no need to worry about feeling deprived or hungry when cooking anymore. With this cookbook, you'll never have another boring meal again!

I know how hard it can be when you have diabetes. That's why I created this air fryer cookbook for party just for diabetics or pre-diabetics like yourself! If you want to simply pay attention to your sugar intake this guide is good , too.

With my help, eating healthy doesn't have to be difficult or boring anymore.

Air fryer cookbook for party is the perfect guide to help you make healthier and tastier meals. It includes recipes that are tailored to your specific situation and goals, with calorie and macronutrient content in mind. You'll get a wide range of nutrients, so it's more likely that you will stick to your diet. Plus, the detailed instructions make meal preparation super simple - no prior cooking experience needed!

Best Recipes Collection

I have been diabetic for five years now, and in this time I have learned that life goes on; it just changes. It's not the end of the world. In fact, with a few precautions I can eat anything! Every morning I wake up to exercise at least 20 minutes before eating breakfast or lunch. Exercise is key because it controls blood sugar levels while preventing future complications like heart attacks or diabetes-related blindness. So what am I going to eat? Any food from my favorite restaurant before 12 pm is okay and after 12 pm however much you want as long as its low glycemic index foods (foods that are absorbed by your body slowly). After following these guidelines for awhile my doctor said "congratulations!" This means that

The best way to prevent hunger pangs in times of unexpected fasting is a well-stocked pantry. Stock up on these items and you'll never be stuck with nothing to eat:

Pasta, rice, canned beans or chickpeas (garbanzo beans), peanut butter, whole wheat bread crusts, frozen vegetables like peas and corn that can go straight from the freezer into boiling water for an easy side dish without any prep work required. No matter how busy life gets it's important not to let your diet suffer because when we're hungry our bodies stop burning fat as efficiently which means weight loss stalls or slows down even more than before!

Pantry List

Have a number of these items on hand at any given time. Use them as main ingredients or supplemental ingredients in your meal, and for snacks too!

Best Recipes Collection

- Apple
- Raspberries
- Loganberries
- Strawberries
- Blueberries
- Wild salmon
- Haddock
- Tuna
- Swordfish
- Mackerel
- Avocados
- Dark chocolate (75% plus)
- Red onions
- Carrots
- Greek yogurt
- Oats
- Cinnamon
- Turmeric
- Leafy greens
- Garlic
- Flaxseed
- Nuts
- Olive oil
- Coconut oil
- Bell peppers
- Black coffee
- Green juice

Why You should choose Air Fryer

If you're looking for a healthier way to cook, an air fryer might be the answer.

Air fryers use hot air instead of oil and can cook everything from french fries (zero calories)to mozzarella sticks (only 8-9 calories per gram!) They can even bake things like pizza rolls or breadsticks with no added butter or oils too. You'll be able to make all your favorite fried foods in less time without any guilt.

Healthy fast food doesn't have to be hard anymore! Get this diabetic Air Fryer cookbook today and start cooking up delicious meals that will satisfy your cravings while still being healthy. This book includes recipes for snacks, appetizers, entrees, desserts and more so there's something for everyone. Plus it comes with a recipe index so you can find what you want quickly and easily.

Order this diabetic Air Fryer cookbook now on our website!

Baking and air frying are two great ways to make nutritious food quickly. Baked goods have a lot less fat than deep fried foods, so they're better for your waistline but just as delicious! The only catch is that baking takes longer than deep frying does - you'll need patience if you want healthy fast food without all the guilt. Air fryers use hot air instead of oil to cook everything from french fries (zero calories)to mozzarella sticks (only 8-9 calories per gram!) They can even bake things like pizza rolls or breadsticks with no added butter or oils too!

Air fryers are the best way to make your kitchen clean. You can put food into a bowl or pot and then cook it in an air fryer, so you do not need big pots or pans at all! Air-fryers also have no limits when cooking with these new devices. They allow anyone from appetizers like fried mozzarella sticks to main dishes like honey baked ham and desserts such as chocolate cakes! These easy recipes that help keep your body healthy will be thought of more often than before because they save time while tasting just right too.*

How much should you eat?

When contemplating portions and combinations of the food groups you will base your diet plan on, try to focus on consuming between 2000-2800 calories a day. Ask your doctor what caloric intake you should be at - adjusting it to factors like exercise level, age and how well diabetes is managed that can play a part in coming up with the perfect figure for yourself!

A well-balanced meal should include a variety of nutrients. You'll get protein, fats, and carbs at every meal if you make use of whole grains like brown rice or quinoa with vegetables such as broccoli or green beans in addition to seafood (or eggs) for your proteins. Fill out the rest of your plate by adding healthy dairy products such as yogurt and cheese that are high in calcium to help keep bones strong while following a plant based diet rich in fiber from veggies like carrots, peppers, cucumbers onion cauliflower; fruits such as berries can also be added for their benefits on heart health!

Best Recipes Collection

Suggested portions for each meal should roughly follow this outline:

➤ ½ plate of non-starchy vegetables - broccoli, green beans, asparagus, peppers, carrots, cucumbers, onions, and cauliflower.
➤ ¼ plate of healthy protein - seafood, eggs, edamame, low fat dairy and yogurt, chicken or turkey, tuna, beans, and soy products (tofu).
➤ ¼ plate carbs - berries, peas, lentils, whole grains (no sugar), oats, quinoa. beans, andsoy products (tofu).

By following this basic outline, you can put together a delicious meal with many varied and flavorful foods. There are also recipes in the book that will let you substitute ingredients to change dishes and your menu! For example, if there aren't any potatoes available for eggs cheese and potato dish, try substituting sweet potatoes or beets instead. Or use zucchini or butternut squash for another delicious variation on the same theme. Don't be afraid to mix things up by moving food groups around as needed!

What is air Fryer?

An air fryer is comparable to the oven in how it roasts and bakes, yet has a distinct difference. The heating elements are situated only on top of an appliance with strong support from a large fan which results in crisp food no time at all. Instead of using pot oil for frying, this unit uses heated spinning air that ensures that hot air flows evenly around your meal without any harm coming its way! It's easy to use too; just place your dinner inside some mesh or racks-- you'll end up with wonderful golden crispy crunch like when fried by the usual means but minus excess grease and fat!

Air fryers have dominated the kitchen appliance market for their ability to make fried food without all of the guilt.

The air fryer is revolutionizing how people cook, as they are doing away with dishes that could be high in fat and calories but still enjoy it just as much!

Cooking with an air fryer is a breeze. You can cook food much faster and easier than the oven or stovetop because of its small size, but it's also super easy to clean up! The heating device at the top provides hot air that moves through and around your food in no time--just like how deep frying works. This fast circulation renders crispy foods just as well without all those messy oils from typical cooking methods so cleanup is really simple too--most systems include dishwasher-safe components for some added convenience.

Tips for Cooking

Shake the basket: open the fryer and move food around while cooking in its tray, squeezing smaller foods such asFrench fries and chips. every 5-10 minutes forbetter performance. Make sure itdoesn't cling to the bowl by gently brushing with a can ofspray cooking oil like Pam or Crisco before you cook it upcrispy (no pun intended). : To preventsplattering and excessive smoke, make sure food is drybefore frying (even if you marinate it. In the same way, besure to remove the grease from the bottom of the machineregularly while preparing high-fat items such as chickenwings.

Best Recipes Collection

101. Lamb Burgers

Servings: 6   Preparation Time: 15 minutes Cooking Time: 8 minutes

Ingredients:

1 1/2 pounds ground lamb

1 tablespoon onion powder

Salt and ground black pepper, as required

In a bowl, add all the ingredients and mix well, make 6 equal-sized patties from the mixture. Arrange the patties onto a cooking tray, arrange the drip pan in the bottom of Instant Vortex Plus Air Fryer Oven cooking chamber. Select "Air Fry" and then adjust the temperature to 360 degrees F., set the timer for 8 minutes and press the "Start". When the display shows "Add Food" insert the cooking rack in the center position, when the display shows "Turn Food" turn the burgers. When cooking time is complete, remove the tray from Vortex and serve hot.

Nutrition: Calories 285   Fat 11.1 g Carbs 0.9 g Protein 42.6 g

102. Lamb Spicy Lemon Kebab

Serves 4   Prep time: 10 minutes Cook time: 30 minutes

Ingredients:

3 tsp lemon juice

2 tsp garam masala

4 tbsp. chopped coriander

3 tbsp. cream

1 lb. of lamb

3 onions chopped

5 green chilies-roughly chopped

1 ½ tbsp. ginger paste

1 ½ tsp garlic paste

1 ½ tsp salt

4 tbsp. fresh mint chopped

3 tbsp. chopped capsicum

3 eggs

2 ½ tbsp. white sesame seeds

Cut the lamb into medium sized chunks. Marinate these chunks overnight in any marinade of your choice. You can use any of the marinades mentioned in this book. Take all the ingredients mentioned under the first heading and mix them in a bowl. Grind them thoroughly to make a smooth paste. Take the eggs in a different bowl and beat them. Add a pinch of salt and leave them aside. Take a flat plate and in it mix the sesame seeds and breadcrumbs. Mold the lamb mixture into small balls and flatten them into round and flat kebabs, dip these kebabs in the egg and salt

Mix all and then in the mixture of breadcrumbs and sesame seeds. Leave these kebabs in the fridge for an hour or so to set. Pre heat the Instant Vortex oven at 160 degrees Fahrenheit for around 5 minutes. Place the kebabs in the basket and let them cook for another 25 minutes at the same temperature. Turn the kebabs over in between the cooking process to get a uniform cook. Serve the kebabs with mint sauce.

Nutrition: Calories 366 Fat 6g Carbs 4g Protein 50 g

103. Lamb Kofta

Serves 4   Prep time: 25 minutes   Cook time: 10 minutes

Special Equipment:

4 bamboo skewers

Ingredients:

1 pound (454 g) ground lamb

1 tablespoon ras el hanout (North African spice)

½ teaspoon ground coriander

2 teaspoon onion powder

2 teaspoon garlic powder

2 teaspoon cumin

2 tablespoons mint, chopped

Salt and ground black pepper, to taste

Directions:

Combine the ground lamb, ras el hanout, coriander, onion powder, garlic powder, cumin, mint, salt, and ground black pepper in a large bowl.

Stir to mix well. Transfer the mixture into sausage molds and sit the bamboo skewers in the mixture.

Refrigerate for 15 minutes, spritz a perforated pan with cooking spray. Place the lamb skewers in the pan and spritz with cooking spray. Select Air Fry of the oven. Set temperature to 380°F (193°C) and set time to 10 minutes. Press Start to begin preheating, once preheated, place the pan into the oven. Flip the lamb skewers halfway through. When cooking is complete, the lamb should be well browned. Serve immediately.

Nutrition: Calories 178 Fat 7.2 g Carbs 27.9 g Protein 1.5 g

104. Easy Lamb Chops With Asparagus

Serves 4　　Prep time: 10 minutes　Cook time: 15 minutes

Ingredients:

4 asparagus spears, trimmed

2 tablespoons olive oil, divided 1 pound (454 g) lamb chops

1　garlic clove, minced

teaspoons chopped fresh thyme, for serving

Salt and ground black pepper, to taste

Spritz a perforated pan with cooking spray, on a large plate, brush the asparagus with 1 tablespoon olive oil, then sprinkle with salt. Set aside. On a separate plate, brush the lamb chops with remaining olive oil and sprinkle with salt and ground black pepper, arrange the lamb chops in the pan. Select Air Fry of the oven. Set temperature to 400°F (205°C) and set time to 15 minutes. Press Start to begin preheating, once preheated, place the pan into the oven. Flip the lamb chops and add the asparagus and garlic halfway through, when cooking is complete, the lamb should be well browned and the asparagus should be tender. Serve them on a plate with thyme on top.

Nutrition:Calories: 324 Protein: 20.2g Carbs: 75.7g Fat: 4.1g

105. Golden Lamb Chops

Serves 4   Prep time: 5 minutes   Cook time: 25 minutes

Ingredients:

1 cup all-purpose flour

2 teaspoons dried sage leaves

2 teaspoons garlic powder

1 tablespoon mild paprika 1 tablespoon salt

4 (6-ounce / 170-g) bone-in lamb shoulder chops, fat trimmed Cooking spray

Spritz a perforated pan with cooking spray. Combine the flour, sage leaves, garlic powder, paprika, and salt in a large bowl. Stir to mix well, dunk in the lamb chops and toss to coat well, arrange the lamb chops in the pan and spritz with cooking spray. Select Air Fry of the oven. Set temperature to 375 degrees F and set time to 25 minutes. Press Start to begin preheating. Once preheated, place the pan into the oven. Flip the chops halfway through, when cooking is complete, the chops should be golden brown and reaches your desired doneness. Serve immediately.

Nutrition: Calories 195 Fat 4.8 g   Carbs 4 g   Protein 35.6 g

106. Lahmacun

Serves 4   Prep time: 20 minutes   Cook time: 10 minutes

Ingredients:

4 (6-inch) flour tortillas For The Meat

Topping:

4 ounces (113 g) ground lamb or 85% lean ground beef

¼ cup finely chopped green bell pepper

¼ cup chopped fresh parsley

1 small plum tomato, deseeded and chopped

2 tablespoons chopped yellow onion

1 garlic clove, minced

2 teaspoons tomato paste

¼ teaspoon sweet paprika

¼ teaspoon ground cumin

⅛ to ¼ teaspoon red pepper flakes

⅛ teaspoon ground allspice

⅛ teaspoon kosher salt

⅛ teaspoon black pepper

For Serving:

¼ cup chopped fresh mint

1 teaspoon extra-virgin olive oil

1 lemon, cut into wedges

Combine all the ingredients for the meat topping in a medium bowl until well mixed. Lay the tortillas on a clean work surface. Spoon the meat mixture on the tortillas and spread all over.

Pork

107. Classic Southern Pork Chops

Serves: 4 Prep Time: 5 mins. Cooking Time: 15 mins.

1/4 cup of all-purpose flour

Salt, to taste

Black pepper, to taste

4 pork chops (bone-in or boneless), 1 pound

3 tablespoon of buttermilk

Ingredients:

Set the Instant Vortex on Air fryer to 380 degrees F for 15 minutes. Season the pork chops with salt and black pepper. Drizzle the chops with buttermilk and sprinkle with the flour. Marinate the chops for about 3 hours. Place the chops in the cooking tray. Insert the cooking tray in the Vortex when it displays "Add Food". Flip the chops when it displays "Turn Food". Remove from the oven when cooking time is complete. Serve hot.

Nutrition: Calories: 548 Protein: 40.1g Carbs: 7.5g   Fat: 22.9g

108. Original Herb Crusted Chops

Serves: 2	Prep Time: 5 mins.	Cooking Time: 15 mins.

Ingredients:

1-pound of pork loin chops bone-in

1 teaspoon of olive oil

1 tablespoon of herb and garlic seasoning

Set the Instant Vortex on Air fryer to 350 degrees F for 14 minutes. Rub the pork chops with oil and seasoning mixture. Place the chops in the cooking tray. Insert the cooking tray in the Vortex when it displays "Add Food". Flip the chops when it displays "Turn Food".

Remove from the oven when cooking time is complete. Serve hot.

Nutrition: Calories: 609 Protein: 23.3g Carbs: 9.9g Fat: 50.5 g

109. Country-Style Pork Ribs

Preparation Time: 5 minutes Cooking Time: 20-25 minutes Servings: 4

Ingredients:

12 country-style pork ribs, trimmed of excess fat 2 tablespoons cornstarch

2 tablespoons olive oil 1 teaspoon dry mustard

½ teaspoon thyme

½ teaspoon garlic powder 1 teaspoon dried marjoram Pinch salt

Freshly ground black pepper, to taste.

Place the ribs on a clean work surface.

In a small bowl, combine the cornstarch, olive oil, mustard, thyme, garlic powder, marjoram, salt, and pepper, and rub into the ribs.

Abode the ribs in the air fryer basket and roast at 400°F (204°C) for 10 minutes.

Carefully turn the ribs using tongs and roast for 10 to 15 minutes or until the ribs are crisp and register an internal temperature of at least 150°F (66°C).

Nutrition: Calories: 579 Fat: 44g Protein: 40g

Carbs: 4g Fibre: 0g Sugar: 0g Sodium: 155mg

110. Dijon Pork Tenderloin

Preparation Time: 10 minutes Cooking Time: 12-14 minutes Servings: 4

Ingredients:

1 pound (454 g) pork tenderloin, cut into

1-inch slices Pinch salt

Freshly ground black pepper, to taste

2 tablespoons Dijon mustard

1 clove garlic, minced

½ teaspoon dried basil

1 cup soft bread crumbs

2 tablespoons olive oil

Slightly pound the pork slices until they are about ¾ inch thick. Sprinkle with salt and pepper on both sides.

Coat the pork with the Dijon mustard and sprinkle with the garlic and basil.

On a plate, combine the bread crumbs and olive oil and mix well. Coat the pork slices with the bread crumb mixture, patting, so the crumbs adhere.

Place the pork in the air fryer basket, leaving a little space between each piece. Air fry at 390°F (199°C) for 12 to 14 minutes or until the pork reaches at least 145°F (63°C) on a meat thermometer and the coating is crisp and brown. Serve immediately.

Nutrition: Calories: 336 Fat: 13g

Protein: 34g Carbs: 20g Fibre: 2g Sugar 2g

Sodium: 390mg

111. Pork Burgers with Red Cabbage Slaw

Preparation Time: 20 minutes Cooking Time: 7-9 minutes Servings: 4

Ingredients:

½ cup Greek yogurt

2 tablespoons low-sodium mustard, divided 1 tablespoon freshly squeezed lemon juice

¼ cup sliced red cabbage

¼ cup grated carrots

1 pound (454 g) lean ground pork

½ teaspoon paprika

1 cup mixed baby lettuce greens 2 small tomatoes, sliced

8 small low-sodium whole-wheat sandwich buns, cut in half

In a lesser bowl, syndicate the yogurt, 1 tablespoon mustard, lemon juice, cabbage, and carrots; mix and refrigerate.

In a medium bowl, combine the pork, remaining 1 tablespoon mustard, and paprika. Form into 8 small patties.

Lay the patties into the air fryer basket. Air fry at 400°F (204°C) for 7 to 9 minutes, or until the patties register 165°F (74°C) as tested with a meat thermometer.

Assemble the burgers by placing some of the lettuce greens on a bun bottom. Top with a tomato slice, the patties, and the cabbage mixture. Add the bun top and serve immediately.

Nutrition: Calories: 473

Fat: 15g Protein: 35g Carbs: 51g Fibre: 8g Sugar: 8g Sodium: 138mg

112. Parmesan-Crusted Pork Loin

Servings: 4   Prep Time: 8 Min   Cooking Time: 20 Minutes

Ingredients:

1 pound pork loin

1 teaspoon salt

1 tablespoons parmesan cheese

1 tablespoon olive oil

1/2 tablespoon garlic powder

1/2 tablespoon onion powder

Start by preheating toaster oven to 475°F., place pan in the oven and let it heat while the oven preheats. Mix all ingredients in a shallow dish and roll the pork loin until it is fully coated. Remove pan and sear the pork in the pan on each side, once seared, bake pork in the pan for 20 minutes. Serve Warm.

Nutrition: Calories: 334 Fat: 20.8 g Carbs: 1.7 g Protein: 33.5 g.

113. Crispy Breaded Pork Chop

Servings: 6　　Prep Time: 10 Min　Cooking Time: 12 Minutes

Ingredients:

olive oil spray

6 3/4-inch thick center-cut boneless pork chops, fat trimmed (5 oz each)

kosher salt

1 large egg, beaten

1 tbsp grated parmesan cheese

1 1/4 tsp sweet paprika

1/2 cup panko crumbs, check labels for GF

1/3 cup crushed cornflakes crumbs

1/2 tsp garlic powder

1/2 tsp onion powder

1/4 tsp chili powder

1/8 tsp black pepper

Preheat the Instant Pot Duo Crisp Air Fryer for 12 minutes at 400°F., on both sides, season pork chops with half teaspoon kosher salt.

Then combine cornflake crumbs, panko, parmesan cheese, 3/4 tsp kosher salt, garlic powder, paprika, onion powder, chili powder, and black pepper in a large bowl, place the egg beat in another bowl. Dip the pork in the egg & then crumb mixture. When the air fryer is ready, place 3 of the chops into the Instant Pot Duo Crisp Air Fryer Basket and spritz the top with oil. Close the Air Fryer lid and cook for 12 minutes turning halfway, spritzing both sides with oil. Set aside and repeat with the remaining.

Nutrition: Calories 281, Fat 13g, Carbs 8g, Protein 33g

114. BBQ Pork Ribs

Servings: 6   Preparation Time: 10 minutes   Cooking Time: 12 minutes

Ingredients:

1 slab baby back pork ribs, cut into pieces

½ cup BBQ sauce

½ tsp paprika Salt

Add pork ribs in a mixing bowl. Add BBQ sauce, paprika, and salt over pork ribs and coat well and set aside for 30 minutes, preheat the instant vortex air fryer oven to 350 F. Arrange marinated pork ribs on instant vortex air fryer oven pan and cook for 10-12 minutes Turn halfway through. Serve and enjoy.

Nutrition: Calories 145 Fat 7 g Carbs 10 g Protein 9 g

115. Super Meatballs

Servings: 8   Preparation Time: 10 minutes   Cooking Time: 12 minutes

Ingredients:

1 lb. ground pork

1 lb. ground beef

1 tbsp Worcestershire sauce

½ cup feta cheese, crumbled

½ cup breadcrumbs

2 eggs, lightly beaten

¼ cup fresh parsley, chopped

1 tbsp garlic, minced

1 onion, chopped

¼ tsp pepper 1 tsp salt

1. Add all ingredients into the mixing bowl and mix until well combined, spray air fryer oven tray pan with cooking spray. Make small balls from meat mixture and arrange on a pan and air fry t 400 F for 10-12 minutes, Serve and enjoy.

Nutrition: Calories 263 Fat 9 g Carbs 7.5 g Protein 35.9 g

115. Seasoned Pork Chops

Servings: 4   Preparation Time: 10 minutes   Cooking Time: 12 minutes

Ingredients:

4 (6-ounce) boneless pork chops

2 tablespoons pork rub

1 tablespoon olive oil

Directions:

Coat both sides of the pork chops with the oil and then, rub with the pork rub, place the pork chops onto the lightly greased cooking tray. Arrange the drip pan in the bottom of Instant Vortex Plus Air Fryer Oven cooking chamber, select "Air Fry" and then adjust the temperature to 400 degrees F. Set the timer for 12 minutes and press the "Start", when the display shows "Add Food" insert the cooking tray in the center position. When the display shows "Turn Food" turn the pork chops, when cooking time is complete, remove the tray from Vortex and serve hot.

Nutrition: Calories 285 Fat 9.5 g Carbs 1.5 g Protein 44.5 g

116. Spiced Pork Shoulder

Servings: 6   Preparation Time: 15 minutes Cooking Time: 55 minutes

Ingredients:

1 teaspoon ground cumin

1 teaspoon cayenne pepper

1 teaspoon garlic powder

Salt and ground black pepper, as required

2 pounds skin-on pork shoulder

In a small bowl, mix together the spices, salt and black pepper, arrange the pork shoulder onto a cutting board, skin-side down. Season the inner side of pork shoulder with salt and black pepper, with kitchen twines, tie the pork shoulder into a long round cylinder shape.

Season the outer side of pork shoulder with spice mixture, insert the rotisserie rod through the pork shoulder. Insert the rotisserie forks, one on each side of the rod to secure the pork shoulder. Arrange the drip pan in the bottom of Instant Vortex Plus Air Fryer Oven cooking chamber, select "Roast" and then adjust the temperature to 350 degrees F. set the timer for 55 minutes and press the "Start". When the display shows "Add Food" press the red lever down and load the left side of the rod into the Vortex. Now, slide the rod's left side into the groove along the metal bar so it doesn't move, then, close the door and touch "Rotate". Press the red lever to release the rod when cooking time is complete, remove the pork from Vortex and place onto a platter for about 10 minutes before slicing. With a sharp knife, cut the pork shoulder into desired sized slices and serve.

Nutrition: Calories 445 Fat 32.5 g Carbs 0.7 g Protein 35.4 g

Lamb

117. Greek Lamb Pita Pockets

Preparation Time: 15 minutes Cooking Time: 5-7 minutes Servings: 4

Ingredients:

Dressing:

1 cup plain Greek yogurt

1 tablespoon lemon juice

1 teaspoon dried dill weed, crushed

1 teaspoon ground oregano

½ teaspoon salt Meatballs:

½ pound (227 g) ground lamb

1 tablespoon diced onion

1 teaspoon dried parsley

1 teaspoon dried dill weed, crushed

¼ teaspoon oregano

¼ teaspoon coriander

¼ teaspoon ground cumin

¼ teaspoon salt

4 pita halves

Suggested Toppings:

Red onion, slivered

Seedless cucumber, thinly sliced

Crumbled feta cheese

Sliced black olives

Chopped fresh peppers

Stir dressing ingredients together and refrigerate while preparing lamb.

Combine all meatball ingredients in a large bowl and stir to distribute seasonings.

Shape meat mixture into 12 small meatballs, rounded or slightly flattened if you prefer.

Air fry at 390°F (199°C) for 5 to 7 minutes, until well done. Remove and drain on paper towels.

To serve, pile meatballs and your choice of toppings in pita pockets and drizzle with dressing.

Nutrition: Calories: 270 Fat: 14g Protein: 18g Carbs: 18g Fibre: 2g Sugar: 2g Sodium: 618mg

118. Crusted Rack Of Lamb

Servings: 4   Preparation Time: 15 minutes   Cooking Time: 19 minutes

Ingredients:

1 rack of lamb, trimmed all fat and frenched

Salt and ground black pepper, as required

1/3 cup pistachios, chopped finely

1 tablespoons panko breadcrumbs

2 teaspoons fresh thyme, chopped finely

1 teaspoon fresh rosemary, chopped finely

1 tablespoon butter, melted

1 tablespoon Dijon mustard

Best Recipes Collection

Insert the rotisserie rod through the rack on the meaty side of the ribs, right next to the bone, insert the rotisserie forks, one on each side of the rod to secure the rack. Season the rack with salt and black pepper evenly, arrange the drip pan in the bottom of Instant Vortex Plus Air Fryer Oven cooking chamber. Select "Air Fry" and then adjust the temperature to 380 degrees F, set the timer for 12 minutes and press the "Start".

When the display shows "Add Food" press the red lever down and load the left side of the

rod into the Vortex, now, slide the rod's left side into the groove along the metal bar so it doesn't move. Then, close the door and touch "Rotate", meanwhile, in a small bowl, mix together the remaining ingredients except the mustard. Press the red lever to release the rod when cooking time is complete, remove the rack from Vortex and brush the meaty side with the mustard. Then, coat the pistachio mixture on all sides of the rack and press firmly, now, place the rack of lamb onto the cooking tray, meat side up. Select "Air Fry" and adjust the temperature to 380 degrees F., set the timer for 7 minutes and press the "Start". When the display shows "Add

Food" insert the cooking tray in the center position, when the display shows "Turn Food" do nothing. When cooking time is complete, remove the tray from Vortex and place the rack onto a cutting board for at least 10 minutes cut the rack into individual chops and serve.

Nutrition: Calories 824   Fat 39.3 g Carbs 10.3 g Protein 72 g

119. Lamb Burgers

Servings: 6   Preparation Time: 15 minutes   Cooking Time: 8 minutes

Ingredients:

1 1/2 pounds ground lamb

1 tablespoon onion powder

Salt and ground black pepper, as required

In a bowl, add all the ingredients and mix well, make 6 equal-sized patties from the mixture. Arrange the patties onto a cooking tray, arrange the drip pan in the bottom of Instant Vortex Plus Air Fryer Oven cooking chamber. Select "Air Fry" and then adjust the temperature to 360 degrees F., set the timer for 8 minutes and press the "Start". When the display shows "Add Food" insert the cooking rack in the center position, when the display shows "Turn Food" turn the burgers. When cooking time is complete, remove the tray from Vortex and serve hot.

Nutrition: Calories 285   Fat 11.1 g Carbs 0.9 g Protein 42.6 g

120. Lamb Spicy Lemon Kebab

Serves 4   Prep time: 10 minutes   Cook time: 30 minutes

Ingredients:

3 tsp lemon juice

2 tsp garam masala

4 tbsp. chopped coriander

3 tbsp. cream

1 lb. of lamb

3 onions chopped

5 green chilies-roughly chopped

1 ½ tbsp. ginger paste

1 ½ tsp garlic paste

1 ½ tsp salt

4 tbsp. fresh mint chopped

3 tbsp. chopped capsicum

3 eggs

2 ½ tbsp. white sesame seeds

Cut the lamb into medium sized chunks. Marinate these chunks overnight in any marinade of your choice. You can use any of the marinades mentioned in this book. Take all the ingredients mentioned under the first heading and mix them in a bowl. Grind them thoroughly to make a smooth paste. Take the eggs in a different bowl and beat them. Add a pinch of salt and leave them aside. Take a flat plate and in it mix the sesame seeds and breadcrumbs. Mold the lamb mixture into small balls and flatten them into round and flat kebabs, dip these kebabs in the egg and salt

mixture and then in the mixture of breadcrumbs and sesame seeds. Leave these kebabs in the fridge for an hour or so to set. Pre heat the Instant Vortex oven at 160 degrees Fahrenheit for around 5 minutes. Place the kebabs in the basket and let them cook for another 25 minutes at the same temperature. Turn the kebabs over in between the cooking process to get a uniform cook. Serve the kebabs with mint sauce.

Nutrition: Calories 366 Fat 6g Carbs 4g Protein 50 g

121. Lamb Kofta

Serves 4   Prep time: 25 minutes   Cook time: 10 minutes

Special Equipment:

4 bamboo skewers

Ingredients:

1 pound (454 g) ground lamb

1 tablespoon ras el hanout (North African spice)

½ teaspoon ground coriander

1 teaspoon onion powder

1 teaspoon garlic powder

1 teaspoon cumin

1 tablespoons mint, chopped

Salt and ground black pepper, to taste

Combine the ground lamb, ras el hanout, coriander, onion powder, garlic powder, cumin, mint, salt, and ground black pepper in a large bowl. Stir to mix well. Transfer the mixture into sausage molds and sit the bamboo skewers in the mixture. Refrigerate for 15 minutes, spritz a perforated pan with cooking spray. Place the lamb skewers in the pan and spritz with cooking spray. Select Air Fry of the oven. Set temperature to 380°F (193°C) and set time to 10 minutes. Press Start to begin preheating, once preheated, place the pan into the oven. Flip the lamb skewers halfway through. When cooking is complete, the lamb should be well browned. Serve immediately.

Nutrition: Calories 178 Fat 7.2 g Carbs 27.9 g Protein 1.5 g

122. Easy Lamb Chops With Asparagus

Serves 4	Prep time: 10 minutes Cook time: 15 minutes

Ingredients:

4 asparagus spears, trimmed

2 tablespoons olive oil, divided

1 pound (454 g) lamb chops

- 1 garlic clove, minced
- 2 teaspoons chopped fresh thyme, for serving Salt and ground black pepper, to taste

Spritz a perforated pan with cooking spray, on a large plate, brush the asparagus with 1 tablespoon olive oil, then sprinkle with salt. Set aside. On a separate plate, brush the lamb chops with remaining olive oil and sprinkle with salt and ground black pepper, arrange the lamb chops in the pan. Select Air Fry of the oven. Set temperature to 400°F (205°C) and set time to 15 minutes. Press Start to begin preheating, once preheated, place the pan into the oven. Flip the lamb chops and add the asparagus and garlic halfway through, when cooking is complete, the lamb should be well browned and the asparagus should be tender. Serve them on a plate with thyme on top.

Nutrition: Calories: 324 Protein: 20.2g Carbs: 75.7g   Fat: 4.1g

123. Golden Lamb Chops

Serves 4　　　　Prep time: 5 minutes　　Cook time: 25 minutes

Ingredients:

1 cup all-purpose flour

2 teaspoons dried sage leaves

2 teaspoons garlic powder

1 tablespoon mild paprika

1 tablespoon salt

4 (6-ounce / 170-g) bone-in lamb shoulder chops, fat trimmed

Cooking spray

Spritz a perforated pan with cooking spray. Combine the flour, sage leaves, garlic powder, paprika, and salt in a large bowl. Stir to mix well, dunk in the lamb chops and toss to coat well, arrange the lamb chops in the pan and spritz with cooking spray. Select Air Fry of the oven. Set temperature to 375 degrees F and set time to 25 minutes. Press Start to begin preheating. Once preheated, place the pan into the oven. Flip the chops halfway through, when cooking is complete, the chops should be golden brown and reaches your desired doneness. Serve immediately.

Nutrition: Calories 195 Fat 4.8 g Carbs 4 g Protein 35.6 g

124. Lamb Loin Chops With Horseradish Cream

Serves 4   Prep time: 10 minutes   Cook time: 13 minutes

Ingredients:

For the Lamb:

900 g. lamb loin chops

2 tablespoons vegetable oil 1 clove garlic, minced

½ teaspoon kosher salt

½ teaspoon black pepper

For the Horseradish Cream Sauce:

1 to 1½ tablespoons prepared horseradish

1 tablespoon Dijon mustard

½ cup mayonnaise 2 teaspoons sugar Cooking spray

Spritz a perforated pan with cooking spray. Place the lamb chops on a plate. Rub with the oil and sprinkle with the garlic, salt and black pepper. Let sit to marinate for 30 minutes at room temperature. Make the horseradish cream sauce: Mix the horseradish, mustard, mayonnaise, and sugar in a bowl until well combined. Set half of the sauce aside until ready to serve, arrange the marinated chops in the perforated pan. Select Air Fry of the oven. Set temperature to 325 degrees F and set time to 10 minutes. Press Start to begin preheating. Once preheated, place the pan into the oven. Flip the lamb chops halfway through, when cooking is complete, the lamb should be lightly browned. Transfer the chops from the oven to the bowl of the horseradish sauce. Roll to coat well. Put the coated chops back in the perforated pan in the oven. Set the temperature to 400 degrees F and the time to 3 minutes, when cooking is complete, the internal temperature should reach 145°F (63°C) on a meat thermometer (for medium-rare). Flip the lamb halfway through. Serve hot with the horseradish cream sauce.

Nutrition: Calories 288 Carbs 1.4g Fat 18.9g Protein 28.3g

125. Lamb Rack With Pistachio

Serves 2 Prep time: 10 minutes Cook time: 20 minutes

Ingredients:

½ cup finely chopped pistachios

1 teaspoon chopped fresh rosemary

3 tablespoons panko breadcrumbs

2 teaspoons chopped fresh oregano

1 tablespoon olive oil

Salt and freshly ground black pepper, to taste

1 lamb rack, bones fat trimmed and frenched

1 tablespoon Dijon mustard

Put the pistachios, rosemary, breadcrumbs, oregano, olive oil, salt, and black pepper in a food processor, pulse to combine until smooth. Rub the lamb rack with salt and black pepper on a clean work surface, then place it in the perforated pan. Select Air Fry of the oven. Set temperature to 380°F (193°C) and set time to 12 minutes. Press Start to begin preheating. Once preheated, place the pan into the oven. Flip the lamb halfway through, when cooking is complete, the lamb should be lightly browned. Transfer the lamb on a plate and brush with Dijon mustard on the fat side, then sprinkle with the pistachios mixture over the lamb rack to coat well, put the lamb rack back to the oven and air fry for 8 more minutes or until the internal temperature of the rack reaches at least 145 degrees F. Remove the lamb rack from the oven with tongs and allow to cool for 5 minutes before slicing to serve.

Nutrition: Calories 212 Fat 7.1 g Carbs 0.4 g Protein 34.5 g

Fish and seafood

127. Tuna Burgers

Serving : 4   Preparation Time: 5 minutes   Cooking Time : 6 minutes

Ingredients:

7 oz canned tuna 1 large egg

¼ cup breadcrumbs 1 tbsp. Mustard

¼ tsp garlic powder

¼ tsp onion powder

¼ tsp cayenne pepper

Salt and ground black pepper, as required

Add all the ingredients into a bowl and mix until well combined. Make 4 equal-sized patties from the mixture. Arrange the patties onto a greased cooking rack. Arrange the drip pan in the bottom of the Instant Vortex Air Fryer Oven cooking chamber. Select "Air Fry" and then adjust the temperature to 400 °F. Set the time for 6 minutes and press "Start". When the display shows "Add Food" insert the cooking rack in the center position. When the display shows "Turn Food" turn the burgers. When the cooking time is complete, remove the tray from the Vortex Oven. Serve hot.

Nutrition: Calories 151 Carbs 6.3g Fat 6.4g Protein 16.4g

128. Flavorful Baked Halibut

Servings: 4   Prep Time: 10 Min   Cooking Time: 12 Minutes

Ingredients:

1 lb halibut fillets

1/4 tsp garlic powder

1/4 tsp paprika

1/4 tsp smoked paprika

1/4 tsp pepper

1/4 cup olive oil

1 lemon juice

1/2 tsp salt

Fit the Instant Vortex oven with the rack in position Place fish fillets into the baking dish. In a small bowl, mix lemon juice, oil, paprika, smoked paprika, garlic powder, and salt. Brush lemon juice mixture over fish fillets, set to bake at 425 F for 17 minutes. After 5 minutes place the baking dish in the preheated oven. Serve and enjoy.

Nutrition: Calories 236 Fat 15.3 g Carbs 0.4 g Protein 24 g

129. Glazed Tuna And Fruit Kebabs

Servings: 4   Prep Time 10 Min   Cooking Time: 10 Minutes

Ingredients:

Kebabs:

1 pound (454 g) tuna steaks, cut into 1-inch cubes

½ cup canned pineapple chunks, drained, juice reserved

½ cup large red grapes

Marinade:

1 tablespoon honey 1 teaspoon olive oil

2 teaspoons grated fresh ginger Pinch cayenne pepper Special Equipment:

4 metal skewers

Make the kebabs: Thread, alternating tuna cubes, pineapple chunks, and red grapes, onto the metal skewers, make the marinade: Whisk together the honey, olive oil, ginger, and cayenne pepper in a small bowl. Brush generously the marinade over the kebabs and allow to sit for 10 minutes. When ready, transfer the kebabs to the air fryer basket. Put the air fryer basket on the baking pan and slide into Rack Position 2, select Air Fry, set temperature to 370 degrees F , and set time to 10 minutes. After 5 minutes, remove from the oven and flip the kebabs and brush with the remaining marinade, return the pan to the oven and continue cooking for an additional 5 minutes, when cooking is complete, the kebabs should reach an internal temperature of 145 degrees F on a meat thermometer. Remove from the oven and discard any remaining marinade. Serve hot.

Nutrition: Calories 168 Carbs 12.1g Fat 2.7g Protein 23.7g

130. Tender & Juicy Cajun Cod

Servings: 6   Prep Time: 15 Min   Cooking Time: 15 Minutes

Ingredients:

3 cod fillets, cut in half 1 tbsp Cajun seasoning 1 tbsp garlic, minced

1 tbsp olive oil

1/4 cup butter, melted Pepper

Salt

Fit the Instant Vortex oven with the rack in position, season fish fillets with pepper and salt and place in a 9*13-inch baking dish. Mix together the remaining ingredients and pour over fish fillets. Set to bake at 400 F for 20 minutes. After 5 minutes place the baking dish in the preheated oven. Serve and enjoy.

Nutrition: Calories 126 Fat 10.4 g Carb 0.5 g Protein 8.2 g

131. Shrimp Skewers

Servings: 4   Prep Time: 10 Min   Cooking Time: 5 Minutes

Ingredients:

1 tbsp. lime juice

1 tbsp. honey

¼ tsp red pepper flakes

¼ tsp pepper

¼ tsp ginger

Nonstick cooking spray

1 lb. medium shrimp, peel, devein & leave tails on 2 cups peaches, drain & chop

½ green bell pepper, chopped fine ¼ cup scallions, chopped

Soak 8 small wooden skewers in water for 15 minutes. In a small bowl, whisk together lime juice, honey and spices. Transfer 2 tablespoons of the mixture to a medium bowl, place the baking pan in position 2 of the oven. Lightly spray fryer basket with cooking spray. Set oven to broil on 400°F for 10 minutes, thread 5 shrimp on each skewer and brush both sides with marinade. Place in basket and after 5 minutes, place on the baking pan. Cook 4-5 minutes or until shrimp turn pink. Add peaches, bell pepper, and scallions to reserved honey mixture, mix well. Divide salsa evenly between serving plates and top with 2 skewers each. Serve immediately.

Nutrition: Calories 181   Fat 1g Carbs 27g   Protein 16g

132. Classic Scallops

Servings: 2   Prep Time: 8 Min   Cooking Time: 4 Minutes

Ingredients:

12 medium sea scallops, rinsed and patted dry

1 teaspoon fine sea salt

¾ teaspoon ground black pepper, plus more for garnish Fresh thyme leaves, for garnish (optional)

Avocado oil spray

Coat the air fryer basket with avocado oil spray. Place the scallops in a medium bowl and spritz with avocado oil spray. Sprinkle the salt and pepper to season, transfer the seasoned scallops to the basket, spacing them apart. Put the air fryer basket on the baking pan and slide into Rack Position 2, select Air Fry, set temperature to 390 degrees F, and set time to 4 minutes, flip the scallops halfway through the cooking time, When cooking is complete, the scallops should reach an internal temperature of just 145°F (63°C) on a meat thermometer. Sprinkle the pepper and thyme leaves on top for garnish, if desired. Serve immediately.

Nutrition: Calories 248 Fat 2.4 g Carbs 12.2 g Protein 44.3 g

133. Spicy Orange Shrimp

Servings: 4   Prep Time: 10 Min   Cooking Time: 12 Minutes

Ingredients:

⅓ cup orange juice

3 teaspoons minced garlic

1 teaspoon Old Bay seasoning

¼ to ½ teaspoon cayenne pepper

1 pound (454 g) medium shrimp, thawed, deveined, peeled, with tails off, and patted dry Cooking spray

Stir together the orange juice, garlic, Old Bay seasoning, and cayenne pepper in a medium bowl. Add the shrimp to the bowl and toss to coat well, cover the bowl with plastic wrap and marinate in the refrigerator for 30 minutes. Spritz the air fryer basket with cooking spray. Place the shrimp in the pan and spray with cooking spray. Put the air fryer basket on the baking pan and slide into Rack Position 2, select Air Fry, set temperature to 400 degrees F, and set time to 12 minutes, flip the shrimp halfway through the cooking time, when cooked, the shrimp should be opaque and crisp. Remove from the oven and serve hot.

Nutrition: Calories 217 Carbs 11.5g Protein 28.0g Fat 10.9g

134. Tasty Parmesan Shrimp

Servings: 4   Prep Time: 10 Min   Cooking Time: 10 Minutes

Ingredients:

1 lb shrimp, peeled and deveined

1/4 cup parmesan cheese, grated

4 garlic cloves, minced

1 tbsp olive oil

1/4 tsp oregano

1/2 tsp pepper

1/2 tsp onion powder

1/2 tsp basil

Fit the Instant Vortex oven with the rack in position 2. Add all ingredients into the large bowl and toss well, add shrimp to the air fryer basket then place an air fryer basket in the baking pan. Place a baking pan on the oven rack. Set to air fry at 350 F for 10 minutes.

Serve and enjoy.

Nutrition: Calories 189 Fat 6.7 g Carbs 3.4 g Protein 27.9 g

135. Seafood Spring Rolls

Servings: 4   Prep Time: 15 Min   Cooking Time: 20 Minutes

Ingredients:

1 tablespoon olive oil

2 teaspoons minced garlic

1 cup matchstick cut carrots

2 cups finely sliced cabbage

2 (4-ounce / 113-g) cans tiny shrimp, drained 4 teaspoons soy sauce

Salt and freshly ground black pepper, to taste 16 square spring roll wrappers

Cooking spray

Spray the air fryer basket with cooking spray. Set aside, heat the olive oil in a medium skillet over medium heat until it shimmers. Add the garlic to the skillet and cook for 30 seconds. Stir in the cabbage and carrots and sauté for about 5 minutes, stirring occasionally, or until the vegetables are lightly tender, fold in the shrimp and soy sauce and sprinkle with salt and pepper, then stir to combine. Sauté for another 2 minutes, or until the moisture is evaporated. Remove from the heat and set aside to cool. Put a spring roll wrapper on a work surface and spoon 1 tablespoon of the shrimp mixture onto the lower end of the wrapper. Roll the wrapper away from you halfway, and then fold in the right and left sides, like an envelope, continue to roll to the very end, using a little water to seal the edge. Repeat with the remaining wrappers and filling. Place the spring rolls in the air fryer basket in a single layer, leaving space between each spring roll, mist them lightly with cooking spray. Put the air fryer basket on the baking pan and slide into Rack Position 2, select Air Fry, set temperature to 375 degrees F , and set time to 10 minutes. Flip the rolls halfway through the cooking time, when cooking is complete, the spring rolls will be heated through and start to brown. If necessary, continue cooking for 5 minutes more. Remove from the oven and cool for a few minutes before serving.

Nutrition: Calories: 220 Protein: 12.8g Carbs: 6g Fat: 17.1g

136. Rosemary Garlic Shrimp

Servings: 4   Prep Time: 8 Min   Cooking Time: 10 Minutes

Ingredients:

1 lb shrimp, peeled and deveined

2 garlic cloves, minced

1/2 tbsp fresh rosemary, chopped

1 tbsp olive oil

Pepper Salt

Fit the Instant Vortex oven with the rack in position, add shrimp and remaining ingredients in a large bowl and toss well. Pour shrimp mixture into the baking dish. Set to bake at 400 F for 15 minutes.

After 5 minutes place the baking dish in the preheated oven. Serve and enjoy.

Nutrition: Calories 168 Fat 5.5 g Carbs 2.5 g Protein 26 g

137. Roasted Halibut Steaks With Parsley

Servings: 4   Prep Time: 10 Min   Cooking Time: 10 Minutes

Ingredients:

1 pound (454 g) halibut steaks

¼ cup vegetable oil

2½ tablespoons Worcester sauce

2 tablespoons honey

2 tablespoons vermouth

1 tablespoon freshly squeezed lemon juice

1 tablespoon fresh parsley leaves, coarsely chopped

Salt and pepper, to taste

1 teaspoon dried basil

Put all the ingredients in a large mixing dish and gently stir until the fish is coated evenly. Transfer the fish to the air fryer basket. Put the air fryer basket on the baking pan and slide into Rack Position 2, select Roast, set temperature to 390 degrees F , and set time to 10 minutes. Flip the fish halfway through cooking time, when cooking is complete, the fish should reach an internal temperature of at least 145 degrees F on a meat thermometer. Remove from the oven and let the fish cool for 5 minutes before serving.

Nutrition: Calories 346 Cal Fat 19.1 g Carbs 20 g Protein 18.5 g

138. Fired Shrimp With Mayonnaise Sauce

Servings: 4   Prep Time: 10 Min   Cooking Time: 7 Minutes

Ingredients:

Shrimp

12 jumbo shrimp

½ teaspoon garlic salt

¼ teaspoon freshly cracked mixed peppercorns

Sauce:

4 tablespoons mayonnaise

1 teaspoon grated lemon rind 1 teaspoon Dijon mustard

1 teaspoon chipotle powder

½ teaspoon cumin powder

In a medium bowl, season the shrimp with garlic salt and cracked mixed peppercorns. Place the shrimp in the air fryer basket. Put the air fryer basket on the baking pan and slide into Rack Position 2, select Air Fry, set temperature to 395degrees F, and set time to 7 minutes. After 5 minutes, remove from the oven and flip the shrimp. Return to the oven and continue cooking for 2 minutes more, or until they are pink and no longer opaque, meanwhile, stir together all the ingredients for the sauce in a small bowl until well mixed. When cooking is complete, remove the shrimp from the oven and serve alongside the sauce.

Nutrition: Calories: 363 Protein: 8.3g Carbs: 35.7g   Fat: 22.5g

139. Greek Cod With Asparagus

Servings: 2   Prep Time: 10 Min   Cooking Time: 20 Minutes

Ingredients:

1 lb cod, cut into 4 pieces

8 asparagus spears

1 leek, sliced

1 onion, quartered

4 tomatoes, halved

1/2 tsp oregano

1/2 tsp red chili flakes

1/2 cup olives, chopped

2 tbsp olive oil

1/4 tsp pepper

1/4 tsp salt

Fit the Instant Vortex oven with the rack in position, arrange fish pieces, olives, asparagus, leek, onion, and tomatoes in a baking dish. Season with oregano, chili flakes, pepper, and salt and drizzle with olive oil. Set to bake at 400 F for 25 minutes. After 5 minutes place the baking dish in the preheated oven. Serve and enjoy.

Nutrition: Calories 489   Fat 20.2 g   Carbs 22.5 g   Protein 56.6 g

140. Halibut Steaks With Parsley

Servings: 4   Prep Time: 10 Min   Cooking Time: 10 Minutes

Ingredients:

1 pound (454 g) halibut steaks

¼ cup vegetable oil

2½ tablespoons Worcester sauce

2 tablespoons honey

2 tablespoons vermouth

1 tablespoon freshly squeezed lemon juice

1 tablespoon fresh parsley leaves, coarsely chopped Salt and pepper, to taste

1 teaspoon dried basil

Put all the ingredients in a large mixing dish and gently stir until the fish is coated evenly. Transfer the fish to the baking pan. Slide the baking pan into Rack Position 1, select Convection Bake, set temperature to 375 degrees F. and set time to 10 minutes. Flip the fish halfway through cooking time, when cooking is complete, the fish should reach an internal temperature of at least 145degrees F , on a meat thermometer. Remove from the oven and let the fish cool for 5 minutes before serving.

Nutrition: Calories 391 Fat 2.8 g Carbs 36.5 g Protein 6.6

141. Roasted Scallops With Snow Peas

Servings: 4   Prep Time: 10 Min   Cooking Time: 8 Minutes

Ingredients:

1 pound (454 g) sea scallops 3 tablespoons hoisin sauce

½ cup toasted sesame seeds

6 ounces (170 g) snow peas, trimmed 3 teaspoons vegetable oil, divided

1 teaspoon soy sauce 1 teaspoon sesame oil

1 cup roasted mushrooms

Brush the scallops with the hoisin sauce. Put the sesame seeds in a shallow dish. Roll the scallops in the sesame seeds until evenly coated, combine the snow peas with 1 teaspoon of vegetable oil, the sesame oil, and soy sauce in a medium bowl and toss to coat.

Grease the baking pan with the remaining 2 teaspoons of vegetable oil. Put the scallops in the middle of the pan and arrange the snow peas around the scallops in a single layer, slide the baking pan into Rack Position 2, select Roast, set temperature to 375°F (190°C), and set time to 8 minutes, after 5 minutes, remove the pan and flip the scallops. Fold in the mushrooms and stir well. Return the pan to the oven and continue cooking, when done, remove from the oven and cool for 5 minutes. Serve warm.

Nutrition: Calories: 374 Protein: 10.2g Carbs: 75.7g   Fat: 2.1g

142. Air Fryer Salmon

Servings: 2 Prep Time: 10 Min Cooking Time: 10 Minutes

Ingredients:

½ tsp. salt

½ tsp. garlic powder

½ tsp. smoked paprika

2 Salmon Fillets

Preparing the Ingredients. Mix spices and sprinkle onto salmon. Place seasoned salmon into the Instant Vortex air fryer oven, Air Frying. Set temperature to 400°F, and set time to 10 minutes.

Nutrition: Calories: 185 Fat: 11g Protein: 21g Carbs: 2g

143. Perfect Baked Cod

Servings: 4   Prep Time: 10 min   Cooking Time: 15 Minutes

Ingredients:

4 cod fillets

1 tbsp olive oil

2 tsp dried parsley 2 tsp paprika

3 jalapeno peppers, seeded & chopped fine

4 6 oz. halibut fillets

3/4 cup parmesan cheese, grated 1/4 tsp salt

Fit the Instant Vortex oven with the rack in position 2, in a shallow dish, mix parmesan cheese, paprika, parsley, and salt. Brush fish fillets with oil and coat with parmesan cheese mixture. Place coated fish fillets into the baking dish. Set to bake at 400 F for 20 minutes. After 5 minutes place the baking dish in the preheated oven. Serve and enjoy.

Nutrition: Calories 160 Fat 8.1 g Carbs 1.2 g Protein 21.7 g

144. Spicy Grilled Halibut

Servings: 4   Prep Time: 5 Min   Cooking Time: 10 Minutes

Ingredients:

½ cup fresh lemon juice

Nonstick cooking spray

¼ cup cilantro, chopped

In a small bowl, combine lemon juice and chilies, mix well, place fish in a large Ziploc bag and add marinade. Toss to coat. Refrigerate 30 minutes. Lightly spray the baking pan with cooking spray. Set oven to broil on 400°F for 15 minutes, after 5 minutes, lay fish on the pan and place in position 2 of the oven. Cook 10 minutes, or until fish flakes easily with a fork. Turn fish over and brush with marinade halfway through cooking time. Sprinkle with cilantro before serving.

Nutrition: Calories 328 Fat 24g Carbs 3g Protein 25g

145. Salmon Beans & Mushrooms

Servings: 6   Time Prep: 10 Min   Cooking Time: 25 Minutes

Ingredients:

2 tbsp fresh parsley, minced

1/4 cup fresh lemon juice

4 salmon fillets

1 tsp garlic, minced 1 tbsp olive oil

1/2 lb mushrooms, sliced

1/2 lb green beans, trimmed

1/2 cup parmesan cheese, grated Pepper

Salt

Fit the Instant Vortex oven with the rack in position Heat oil in a small saucepan over medium-high heat. Add garlic and sauté for 30 seconds, remove from heat and stir in lemon juice, parsley, pepper, and salt. Arrange fish fillets, mushrooms, and green beans in baking pan and drizzle with oil mixture. Sprinkle with grated parmesan cheese. Set to bake at 400 F for 30 minutes. After 5 minutes place the baking pan in the preheated oven. Serve and enjoy.

Nutrition: Calories 225   Fat 11.5 g Carbs 4.7 g Protein 27.5 g

146. Salmon Cakes

Servings: 2　　Prep Time: 10 Min　　Cooking Time: 15 Minutes + Cooling Time

Ingredients:

8 oz salmon, cooked

1 ½ oz potatoes, mashed A handful of capers

A handful of parsley, chopped Zest of 1 lemon 1 ¾ oz plain flour

Carefully flake the salmon in a bowl. Stir in zest, capers, dill, and mashed potatoes. Shape the mixture into cakes and dust them with flour. Place in the fridge for 60 minutes. Preheat your Instant Vortex to 350 F on Air Fry function. Remove the cakes from the fridges and arrange them on the greased basket. Fit in the baking tray and cook for 10 minutes, shaing once halfway through. Serve chilled.

Nutrition : Calories 472 Fat 25.8 g Carbs 1.7 g Protein 59.6 g

147. Lobster Lemon Kebab

Servings: 2　　Prep Time: 5 Min　Cooking Time: 10 Minutes

Ingredients:

1 lb. lobster (Shelled and cubed)

3 onions chopped

5 green chilies-roughly chopped

1 ½ tbsp. ginger paste

1 ½ tsp garlic paste 1 ½ tsp salt

3 tsp lemon juice

2 tsp garam masala

4 tbsp. chopped coriander

3 tbsp. cream

2 tbsp. coriander powder

4 tbsp. fresh mint chopped

3 tbsp. chopped capsicum

3 eggs

2 ½ tbsp. white sesame seeds

Take all the ingredients mentioned under the first heading and mix them in a bowl. Grind them thoroughly to make a smooth paste. Take the eggs in a different bowl and beat them. Add a pinch of salt and leave them aside. Take a flat plate and in it mix the sesame seeds and breadcrumbs, dip the lobster cubes in the egg and salt mixture and then in the mixture of breadcrumbs and sesame seeds. Leave these kebabs in the fridge for an hour or so to set. Pre heat the Instant Vortex oven at 160 degrees Fahrenheit for around 5 minutes.

Place the kebabs in the basket and let them cook for another 25 minutes at the same temperature. Turn the kebabs over in between the cooking process to get a uniform cook. Serve the kebabs with mint sauce.

Nutrition: Calories: 253 Protein: 13.1g Carbs: 10.4g   Fat: 7.5g

148. Fish Spicy Lemon Kebab

Servings: 2   Prep Time: 5 Min   Cooking Time: 10 Minutes

Ingredients:

1 lb. boneless fish roughly chopped

3 onions chopped

5 green chilies-roughly chopped

1 ½ tbsp. ginger paste

1 ½ tsp garlic paste

1 ½ tsp salt

3 tsp lemon juice

2 tsp garam masala

4 tbsp. chopped coriander

3 tbsp. cream

2 tbsp. coriander powder

146. Salmon Cakes

Servings: 2   Prep Time: 10 Min   Cooking Time: 15 Minutes + Cooling Time

Ingredients:

8 oz salmon, cooked

1 ½ oz potatoes, mashed A handful of capers

A handful of parsley, chopped Zest of 1 lemon 1 ¾ oz plain flour

Carefully flake the salmon in a bowl. Stir in zest, capers, dill, and mashed potatoes. Shape the mixture into cakes and dust them with flour. Place in the fridge for 60 minutes. Preheat your Instant Vortex to 350 F on Air Fry function. Remove the cakes from the fridges and arrange them on the greased basket. Fit in the baking tray and cook for 10 minutes, shaing once halfway through. Serve chilled.

Nutrition : Calories 472 Fat 25.8 g Carbs 1.7 g Protein 59.6 g

147. Lobster Lemon Kebab

Servings: 2   Prep Time: 5 Min   Cooking Time: 10 Minutes

Ingredients:

1 lb. lobster (Shelled and cubed)

3 onions chopped

5 green chilies-roughly chopped

1 ½ tbsp. ginger paste

1 ½ tsp garlic paste 1 ½ tsp salt

3 tsp lemon juice

2 tsp garam masala

4 tbsp. chopped coriander

3 tbsp. cream

2 tbsp. coriander powder

4 tbsp. fresh mint chopped

3 tbsp. chopped capsicum

4 tbsp. fresh mint chopped

3 tbsp. chopped capsicum

3 eggs

2 ½ tbsp. white sesame seeds

Take all the ingredients mentioned under the first heading and mix them in a bowl. Grind them thoroughly to make a smooth paste. Take the eggs in a different bowl and beat them. Add a pinch of salt and leave them aside. Take a flat plate and in it mix the sesame seeds and breadcrumbs. Mold the fish mixture into small balls and flatten them into round and flat kebabs. Dip these kebabs in the egg and salt mixture and then in the mixture of breadcrumbs and sesame seeds. Leave these kebabs in the fridge for an hour or so to set. Pre

heat the Instant Vortex oven at 160 degrees Fahrenheit for around 5 minutes. Place the kebabs in the basket and let them cook for another 25 minutes at the same temperature. Turn the kebabs over in between the cooking process to get a uniform cook. Serve the kebabs with mint sauce.

Nutrition: Calories 90 Fat 4.5g Carbs 8g Protein 13g

149. Coconut Shrimp

Servings: 4　　Prep Time: 10 Min　Cooking Time: 5 Minutes

Ingredients:

1 (8-ounce) can crushed pineapple ½ cup sour cream

¼ cup pineapple preserves 2 egg whites

⅔ cup cornstarch

⅔ cup sweetened coconut 1 cup panko bread crumbs

1 pound uncooked large shrimp, thawed if frozen, deveined and shelled Olive oil for misting

Preparing the Ingredients. Drain the crushed pineapple well, reserving the juice. In a small bowl, combine the pineapple, sour cream, and preserves, and mix well. Set aside. In a shallow bowl, beat the egg whites with 2 tablespoons of the reserved pineapple liquid. Place the cornstarch on a plate. Combine the coconut and bread crumbs on another plate. Dip the shrimp into the cornstarch, shake it off, then dip into the egg white mixture and finally into the coconut mixture. Place the shrimp in the air fryer rack/basket and mist with oil. Air-fry mode for 5 to 7 minutes or until the shrimp are crisp and golden brown.

Nutrition: Calories: 524; Fat: 14g; Protein:33g; Carbs:2g

150. Lemon Salmon

Servings: 2   Prep Time: 10 Min   Cooking Time: 20 Minutes

Ingredients:

2 salmon fillets Salt to taste Zest of 1 lemon

Rub the fillets with salt and lemon zest. Place them in the frying basket and spray with cooking spray. Press Start and cook the salmon in the preheated Instant Vortex oven for 14 minutes at 360 F on AirFry function. Serve with steamed asparagus and a drizzle of lemon juice.

Nutrition: Calories: 695   Protein: 17.4g Carbs: 6.4g Fat: 17.5g

My Secrets To Get Better Dishes and… Extra Crunchies

Do you want to know how to get extra crunchies?

You've come to the right place. I have a few tricks up my sleeve that will make your food taste better and be healthier than ever before. These are some of my secrets for getting better dishes and more crunchies, crispies.

If you follow these tips, you can enjoy all the benefits of eating healthy without giving up any flavor or texture. And don't worry about feeling deprived because this is not a diet - it's just a way of life!

What Other Air Fryer Lovers Don't know...

- Use olive oil instead of butter in recipes

- Add spices like garlic powder or cayenne pepper to foods for an added kick

- Make sure your pan is hot enough when cooking so that the food doesn't stick and burn on the bottom

- Cook vegetables with high water content first (like onions) then add other vegetables later on in the process so they don't get too soggy from sitting in liquid too long while waiting their turn at being cooked

- When baking cookies, use parchment paper instead of greasing pans because it makes them easier to remove from the pan after baking without breaking apart into pieces which means less clean up time!

- For pancakes, use whole wheat flour instead of white flour which has been processed many times over and has lost most nutrients by now; also try adding cinnamon or vanilla extract for an even tastier dish

1. A rotisserie is a marvelous invention that can save you time in the kitchen. The only downside to this cooking tool is forgetting what's going on once it starts turning! When using a rotisserie, always put your food before touching the Start button so as not to forget anything else when everything moves around.

2. For those of us who don't enjoy the taste or texture of overcooked food, it is important to keep an eye on our cooking time. Fortunately there's a simple way to avoid this: cover your dish with foil! This will help you from over-cooking and ensure that all parts come out tender and juicy when served. Remember not get too close so as not let steam burn your skin!

3. There are many different ways to cook food, but if you don't want any hassle it's best just to oven-bake them. All the other cooking methods can be done well with an activated oven and a little patience. After activating your oven (and waiting for its temperature gauge), add some fresh ingredients - veggies or meat of choice will do nicely! Let your meal fully bake on medium heat before taking out so that every last bit is cooked through satisfactorily. But what about rotisserie chicken? Well, since all these foods need only one heating point from which they spread their flavors evenly throughout the dish, in short order there'll be nothing left not too dry up...no siree "broiling" isn't necessary either.

4. It's always a good idea to dry your foods before you start cooking them, especially in the air fryer oven. If excess steam and splatter are left unchecked for too long it can leave a mess on any nearby surfaces such as countertops or linens."

5. However... not all of the food that you cook in an air-fryer needs to be dried. But, if there is a chance it will get too wet for your liking or cause any splattering on the inside walls then by all means dry it first!

6. Spraying cooking oil on your food can help it develop a more delicious flavor. Cooks and chefs have been doing this for centuries, but you don't need to be an expert cook in order to

7. enjoy the benefits of using cooking oils as seasoning agents!

8. To make fries crispy and golden, put potatoes in cold water for 15 minutes. Dry them off, then spray with some oil before putting them into an oven that is heated to 400 degrees Fahrenheit.

MEASUREMENT CONVERSION

VOLUME EQUIVALENTS (DRY)

US STANDARD	METRIC (APPROXIMATE)
1/8 teaspoon	0.5 mL
1/4 teaspoon	1 mL
1/2 teaspoon	2 mL
3/4 teaspoon	4 mL
1 teaspoon	5 mL
1 tablespoon	15 mL
1/4 cup	59 mL
1/2 cup	118 mL
3/4 cup	177 mL
1 cup	235 mL
2 cups	475 mL
3 cups	700 mL
4 cups	1 L

VOLUME EQUIVALENTS (LIQUID)

US STANDARD	US STANDARD (OUNCES)	METRIC (APPROXIMATE)
2 tablespoons	1 fl.oz.	30 mL
1/4 cup	2 fl.oz.	60 mL
1/2 cup	4 fl.oz.	120 mL
1 cup	8 fl.oz.	240 mL
1 1/2 cup	12 fl.oz.	355 mL
2 cups or 1 pint	16 fl.oz.	475 mL
4 cups or 1 quart	32 fl.oz.	1 L
1 gallon	128 fl.oz.	4 L

TEMPERATURES EQUIVALENTS

FAHRENHEIT(F)	CELSIUS(C) (APPROXIMATE)
225 °F	107 °C
250 °F	120 °C
275 °F	135 °C
300 °F	150 °C
325 °F	160 °C
350 °F	180 °C
375 °F	190 °C
400 °F	205 °C
425 °F	220 °C
450 °F	235 °C
475 °F	245 °C
500 °F	260 °C

WEIGHT EQUIVALENTS

US STANDARD	METRIC (APPROXIMATE)
1 ounce	28 g
2 ounces	57 g
5 ounces	142 g
10 ounces	284 g
15 ounces	425 g
16 ounces (1 pound)	455 g
1.5 pounds	680 g
2 pounds	907 g

Conclusion

Diabetic Air-Fryer Cookbook cookware is not just for diabetic air fryers, it also cooks your food evenly and quickly so you can enjoy more time to talk with the people around you. It's durable and nonstick which means that after each use there will be no scrubbing needed - all of this without sacrificing quality or cleanliness when cooking; what could make a meal better?

A Diabetic Air-Fryer Cookbook air fryer is an easy way to cook healthy food, and they are great for one-hand operation. They also have a reversible stainless steel handle so you can carry it on your hip or in your hand!

There are a lot of unhealthy food options on the market today. For those with diabetes or who don't have much time, cooking is challenging because it's hard to make healthy fast foods. This Cookbook was written specifically for these people and can help them learn how to cook safely so they can enjoy their favorite dishes without risking health complications in the future.

The guide is the perfect way to ensure that you never worry about your diet again. It contains all of the recipes and instructions for how to prepare healthy meals during a fast or when suffering from diabetes.

It is a difficult task to cook for someone with diabetes. You would be wise not only in following the instructions carefully but also put into consideration some tips so that you can prepare healthy dishes and foods without making anyone feel like they're being deprived of flavor or restrictions on their diet.

Enjoy it!

Best Recipes Collection

www.ingramcontent.com/pod-product-compliance
Lightning Source LLC
Chambersburg PA
CBHW080628170426
43209CB00007B/1537